CW01072292

VERSES FROM THE HEART

Edited By Lynsey Evans

First published in Great Britain in 2024 by:

Young Writers
Remus House
Coltsfoot Drive
Peterborough
PE2 9BF
Telephone: 01733 890066
Website: www.youngwriters.co.uk

Printed and bound in the UK by BookPrintingUK
Website: www.bookprintinguk.com
YB0574J

FOREWORD

For Young Writers' latest competition This Is Me,
we asked primary school pupils to look inside
themselves, to think about what makes them unique,
and then write a poem about it! They rose to the
challenge magnificently and the result is this fantastic
collection of poems in a variety of poetic styles.

Here at Young Writers our aim is to encourage creativity
in children and to inspire a love of the written word, so
it's great to get such an amazing response, with some
absolutely fantastic poems. It's important for children to
focus on and celebrate themselves and this competition
allowed them to write freely and honestly, celebrating
what makes them great, expressing their hopes and
fears, or simply writing about their favourite things.
This Is Me gave them the power of words. The result
is a collection of inspirational and moving poems that
also showcase their creativity and writing ability.

I'd like to congratulate all the young poets
in this anthology, I hope this inspires them
to continue with their creative writing.

CONTENTS

Ingrid Girjoaba (10)	73	Areebah Ahmed (11)	122
Zoya Ali (8)	74	Hawwa Ibrahim (11)	123
Alec Morgan (7)	75	Umme-Khair Faatimah (11)	124
Anna Bottoni (9)	76	Sawda Zainab (12)	125
Cerinda Sirichantaropass (11)	77	Halima Khan (12)	126
Rahini Didwania (7)	78	Laiba Abas (11)	127
Sara Saoji (8)	79	Hafsah Bismillah (11)	128
Anna Bhagalee (7)	80	Sajida Ali (11)	129
Constance Gillespie (7)	81	Aaidah Suhail (12)	130
Leo Purnomo (8)	82	Hajira Shehriyar (11)	131
Amy Grandison (7)	83	Aaila Zaman (11)	132
Rudra Shembekar (9)	84	Imaan Fatimah (11)	133
Jessica Swayze (7)	85	Aysha Memi (11)	134
Josie Barnbrook (9)	86	Fareeha Ashraf (11)	135
Isabel Sims (7)	87	Muniba Khan (11)	136
Amelia Singleton (9)	88	Khadija Javed (11)	137
		Laiba Abas (11)	138

Feversham Girls' Secondary Academy, Undercliffe

		Ghaaziyah Rizwan (11)	139
		Zarrah Kabil (11)	140
		Youmna Hamed (11)	141
Rania Abdelrahim (11)	89	Inayah Mahmood (12)	142
Arooj Iqbal (11)	90	Safiyah Bint Ahmad (11)	143
Zaynah Hans (11)	92	Maryam Zeeshan (11)	144
Aliyah Mahmood (11)	95	Marwa Nadeem (11)	145
Hawwa Ahsan (11)	96	Fatima Zahra (11)	146
Aisha Siddiqa (12)	98		
Arfa Tahir (11)	100		

Ruskin Academy, Wellingborough

Hawwa Nawaz (11)	102		
Haniya Nazir (11)	103	Tiana Weston (10)	147
Zakia Mohammed (11)	104	Twisha Patel	148
Hifza Nadeem (11)	106	Oliwia Dziecielska (10)	149
Amirah Hassan (11)	108	Caira-Jae Hill (10)	150
Leia Omer (11)	109	Oceana Munton (10)	151
Ayesha Patel (11)	110	Patricia Zdrinca (10)	152
Hafsa Asif (11)	111	James Coe-Welch (10)	153
Ayesha Waseem Attaria (11)	112	Martyna Grobelna (9)	154
Anbar Saeed (11)	113	Maia Rickett-Browne (10)	155
Zahra Ahmed (11)	114	Cleopatra Leon (9)	156
Mariam Khan (11)	115	Emri Johnson (8)	157
Inaaya Rizwan (12)	116	Zyla Agyemang (8)	158
Huriyah Khan (11)	117	Lakiyra Morris	159
Raihana Qudratullah	118	Jessica-Rose Stiller (7)	160
Sofia Ali (12)	120		
Hibba Hussain (11)	121		

Woodlands School, Great Warley

Leonardo Spurling (8)	161
Demi Brown (7)	162
Fleur Basi (7)	163
Esmé Burchell (8)	164
Opal Adams (7)	165
Lucia Everson (7)	166
Chloe Wedderburn (7)	167
Izzy Andrews (7)	168
Adarsh Vemula (7)	169
Timmy Tudor (7)	170
Ranuka Gunaratne (7)	171
Kennedy Cullen (7)	172
Öykü Akcan (7)	173
Shreya Singh (8)	174

Ysgol Bryn Hedydd, Rhyl

Abigail Thomas (10)	175
Elin Mathews (10)	176
Chloe Jones (10)	178
Sadie Schofield (10)	180
Zachary MacClelland (10)	181
Freya Heeley (10)	182
Lily Goddard (10)	183
Lilly-May Bullingham (10)	184
Seren Jane Rastin (10)	185
Rose Ashley (10)	186
Erin Smith (10)	187
Dylan Bailey (10)	188
Jacob Bellis (11)	189

THE POEMS

Christmas Poem

My name is Victory and I love Christmas
It is so fun
It is the best day
I love December, it is always snowy
It is always cold and cosy
I want to invite all my friends for Christmas
It is a happy day
We were playing
We love playing with snow
Christmas is the best day
At Christmas, I went to a party at 10 o'clock in the morning
And Santa Claus had visited
And he was throwing candies around, all over the ground
I was so, so, so excited I could've burst
My head erupted like a volcano
And I was telling my mum all about Christmas.

Victory Olawuni Treasure (8)
Ashley Road Primary School, Aberdeen

My Life

N ancy is nice like a dog.

A pples are my favourite fruit.

N ever stopping to give up.

C lever and sneaky like a cat.

Y oghurt is my favourite food for breakfast.

M itova is my last name.

I vilova is my second name.

T alking to my friends gives me a smile on my face.

O live is my friend.

V iolin is my least favourite instrument.

A cake is my favourite dessert.

Nancy Mitova (8)

Ashley Road Primary School, Aberdeen

My Life

M y life is the best
Y es I will never give up

L ove myself
I love my family
F elicity is my friend
E verybody has rights

I love myself
S how the world what you can be

G irls have opportunities
R ights are for everyone
E verybody should be treated equally
A sk for help if you need it
T o be great for who I am.

Rebecca Ortecho (8)
Ashley Road Primary School, Aberdeen

My Life With Friends

In my house, my friends munched
And crunched the tasty food.
Bang went the door,
It was so loud and scary.

I saw a dark and scary bear,
Growling like we were its dinner.
A knight as brave as a dragon arrived.
He touched the bear
And in an instant, it disappeared.

I smelt something quite exquisite.
As I turned my head,
A pancake was in my hands.
In the end, I ate the pancake.

Chiamaka Agbogu (8)
Ashley Road Primary School, Aberdeen

My Life!

My friends are as nice as ice cream
On my head is my hair
And swoosh it goes in the wind

I have a brother who is
Two years older than me
My mother is as sweet as roses
I love doughnuts, bananas and me.
A sweet, sweet dad I own forever

I will always remember how lucky I am
Playing games to writing books
I love it all, I love my life
And that's the point of this poem.

Morgane Emeriau (8)
Ashley Road Primary School, Aberdeen

Elliot's Life

My name is Elliot
I like a lot of stuff
I like football
I like Liverpool, Aberdeen and Arsenal
I want to live in Greece.
And my favourite food is Chinese chicken,
Curry and tomato pasta.
Next I had a dog called Magie
And Lola and Amber.
I like golfing and I go to a golfing lesson
On a Friday
But this Friday I am not going to it
Because I am going
To Italy this week.

Elliot Artair Powell (7)
Ashley Road Primary School, Aberdeen

My Life

E dith is my name, I am kind and helpful

D ogs, bunnies and cats are my favourite animals

I am eight years old

T alking to my friends always puts a smile on my face

H ot weather is my favourite

L emons are sour

U p the stairs in school is so tiring

N ancy is my friend

D inosaurs are extinct.

Edith Lund (8)

Ashley Road Primary School, Aberdeen

My Great Life

M y life is a really good one.
Y early it is my birthday.

G reat bangs and pops I like.
R oller blades are fun.
E veryone is awesome.
A house is nice.
T he world is amazing.

L ife is good.
I am very happy.
F lips are fun.
E verybody is different.

Thomas Redvers (8)
Ashley Road Primary School, Aberdeen

What Festival Is This?

You get presents on this day
There's a tree as big as a slide
You celebrate it with your family
Jesus was born on this day
I like the festival very much
I wake up early on this day
We wear special hats
The festival is exciting - I jump all day
The day before we eat a feast
The festival is fun - I like it
What is this festival?

Adriana Kong (8)
Ashley Road Primary School, Aberdeen

This Is Me!

I like slime
Limes are sour
And I like running
I also like cooking
I love cars
And Transformers
I like red like on the planet Mars
I love colouring
I also like drawing
I absolutely love doughnuts
I also like nuts.

Ivy Uchechi (8)
Ashley Road Primary School, Aberdeen

My Life

M y life is amazing,
Y ears are all different,

L ife is precious,
I 'm great and so is everyone else,
F eelings should be shared,
E veryone is different.

Callum Lourie (7)

Ashley Road Primary School, Aberdeen

All About Me, Alanna

A lanna is my name.
L ike bananas as much as a monkey.
A dventures are fun, I like them.
N ice to know me.
N ice with resilience.
A nice friend to have.

Alanna Simpson (8)
Ashley Road Primary School, Aberdeen

This Is Me!

A ydan is my name.

Y es, I like cycling.

D oughnuts are my favourite food.

A shley Road is my school.

N oodles are yummy.

Aydan Semmane (7)

Ashley Road Primary School, Aberdeen

Emotion Me (Guess The Emotion)

Hearing game noises
Feeling the sofa on me
Being comfy
Playing Designer City
2,000 people
With boring noises
Hearing narrator voices
The Angry Game.

Bruno Chmiel (7)

Ashley Road Primary School, Aberdeen

A Recipe To Make Me

Ingredients:
555 tons of green
5tsp of stick insects
66 slices of foxy
A squeeze of drakes
2 1/2 violins
6 slices of video games
A pinch of fearlessness
15 hints of Pokémon
6kg of pasta

Method:
1. First measure out all the ingredients
2. Then add 555 tons of green to the bowl
3. Whisk roughly while adding in 2 1/2 violins
4. Squeeze in a drake (Warning: *Hot!!*)
5. Add in a pinch of fearlessness and mix for 6 minutes
6. Mix in everything else and blend roughly
7. Finally bake for 8 years and you have a perfect *me!*

Olivia Levick (8)
Barlborough Hall School, Barlborough

A Recipe To Make Me

Ingredients:
A dash of smartness
A sprinkle of stinkiness
A slice of pizza or two
A cup of drawing
A jug of history
One thousand cuddles
Two kilograms of video games
A bucket of silliness
A slice of helping
A piece of hockey
One kilogram of an author
A pinch of eating
500 grams of fear.

Method:
First, put the dash of smartness and the sprinkle of silliness into a large bowl.
Next, add the cup of drawing and the slices of pizza and pour the jug of history into the bowl.
Then cuddle the bowl one thousand times so that the cuddles go into the mixture.

Put the video games into the bowl with the bucket of silliness.

Drop the slice of helping in with a piece of hockey.

Add one kilogram of the author, making sure you don't drop any of it.

Finally, add a pinch of eating and 500 grams of fear.

Don't eat any of it yet.

Mix it up with a wooden spoon, but don't get any splinters in the mixture, or it might come out made of wood.

Pour it into a big pan and put on the lid.

Put it into the oven to cook for eight seconds, sometimes eight minutes, sometimes eight days, sometimes eight months and sometimes eight years.

Or, if you don't have an oven, it will be eight centuries.

Arthur Regi (8)

Barlborough Hall School, Barlborough

A Recipe To Make Me

Ingredients:
One gram of penguin
One kilogram of foxes
Ten grams of dogs
One hundred grams of dinosaurs
Five grams of pizza
Five grams of hockey
One kilogram of reading
Five cups of hot chocolate
A pinch of Pokémon

Method:
1. First put one gram of penguin in the bowl then add one kilogram of foxes
2. Next add ten grams of dogs and stir for one minute
3. Add 100 grams of dinosaur to the mixture and whisk for one minute
4. Then add five grams of pizza and five grams of hockey and stir slowly for five minutes
5. Pour the five cups of hot chocolate and carefully stir for a further ten minutes then add the pinch of Pokémon

6. Finally add one kilogram of reading and bake in the oven for eight years
7. Remove and place on a cooling tray for three quarters of a year
8. Now you have the perfect me... enjoy!

Johnny Grice (8)
Barlborough Hall School, Barlborough

What You Need To Make Me

Ingredients:
A bed of joy.
A dog or cat full of excitement.
A mum or dad of happiness.
Nice clothes.
A breakfast of fanciness.
Curiosity.
Four cups of love.
Pour the cups of love into the breakfast.
Add a cup of apple juice.
Pack my bag with kindness.

The recipe about me:
First, jump out of the bed of joy.
Next, wake up the dog or cat in excitement.
Then, wake up the mum or dad with happiness.
Get dressed in nice clothes.
After that, have a breakfast of fanciness.
Sprinkle the day with curiosity.
Get four cups of love.

Pour the four cups of love onto your breakfast.
Add a cup of apple juice to the cup of joy.
Pack my bag of kindness for school.

Ivy Wilbraham (8)
Barlborough Hall School, Barlborough

A Recipe To Make Me

Ingredients:
6tsp of dogs
15tbsp of foxes
500g of fun
1kg Pokémon
5 slices of chocolate
A sprinkle of happiness
A squeeze of spaghetti bolognese
5 pieces of piano
A sprinkle of silliness
9g of holidays
50tbsp of school

Method:
1. Gather the ingredients
2. Then grab 6tsp of dogs
3. Get five pieces of piano
4. Squeeze some spaghetti bolognese
5. A sprinkle of happiness and silliness
6. Put five pieces of chocolate in to make it sweet
7. Add 1kg of Pokémon

8. Stir in 9g of holidays

9. Whisk in 50tbsp of school until the perfect consistency

10. Bake for eight years

11. Enjoy your Alaya.

Alaya Akbar (8)

Barlborough Hall School, Barlborough

My Recipe Poem

Ingredients:
1 cup of happiness
3tsp of hamster
8g of athletics
1/2 a cup of kindness
A sprinkle of family
A squeeze of teddy
10,000 cups of craziness
10 cups of cross-country
9,000tbsp of curry
Chop up 5g of hockey

Method:
1. Get the ingredients
2. Mix kindness and happiness and pour it in a bowl
3. Stir them together
4. Then add craziness
5. Next add 9g of hamster
6. After get the sprinkle of family
7. Next add the 3tsp of hamster
8. Then stir it

9. After add the squeezed teddy

10. Next add the 8g of athletics and then bake for 8 years.

Millie Colclough (8)

Barlborough Hall School, Barlborough

This Is Me, Bea

My passions are netball, music and art.
I love my friends, I hope we never grow apart.
My favourite flower is probably a daisy.
My favourite animal is a monkey.
Pure orange juice cannot be beaten.
Same as my grandma's home-made quiche.
Blue and pink are my favourite colours.
They make me feel like me!
I'm very proud to be the athletics captain at school.
But I find it hard to keep it cool.
I love being kind and seeing people happy.
I get lost in books and listening to pop music.
These are a few things I like, but there are loads more!
This is me, Bea!

Beatrice Challinor-Moss (11)
Barlborough Hall School, Barlborough

What Makes Me

I like to play tennis,
But it makes me a menace.

In rugby, when I score a try,
It makes the other team cry.

I am the best in my year group at cricket,
Because I always aim the ball at the wicket.

I call my friends 'dude',
When I feel in the mood.

I look after my health,
To help myself.

I normally feel worried,
When I am being bullied.

When I am helpful,
I am also very grateful.

My life is exciting,
Because of the poem I am writing.

Sehj Nijjar (7)
Barlborough Hall School, Barlborough

All About Me

My favourite colour is yellow, shining as bright as the sun.
Food, you ask me, let's think; pizza, fish and chips, and don't forget fajitas!
Now, let's move on to my favourite lesson.
I love school! But do I have to pick one lesson?
Maths, it will be!
I like most things out of school, but my favourite is baking.
My hobbies are Forest School, STEM and computing.
I don't like many sports but I do like some.
Hockey, swimming and gymnastics are my pick!
My name is Matilda and I am seven years old!

Matilda Draper (7)
Barlborough Hall School, Barlborough

This Is Me

I love dogs and Depeche Mode,
Lifelong Leeds fan,
Amazing at accents,
Man United are rivals,
So are Chelsea,
My family is very crucial to me,
I don't like coffee, but I love a cup of tea,
I'm a fan of Alan Shearer, Kevin Phillips, Gazza and more,
Pasta is my favourite food,
Two older sisters are amazing of course,
Sport is my passion, but don't forget FIFA,
I'm Jamie Carragher or Dom Matteo in defence,
Elland Road is my home,
I am William Jones.

William Jones (10)
Barlborough Hall School, Barlborough

A Recipe To Create Me

You will need:
Lots of books
Lots of animals
My family
A pencil and pen
A dollop of friends
Fun and laughter
Pizza

How to make me:
Add five teaspoons of fun and laughter
Mix hard and add lots of books
Start mixing gently and slowly
Add lots of animals
Quickly throw a dollop of friends and family in
Drop a pencil and pen in
Pour it into a tray
Plop a piece of cheesy pizza on top
Leave to cool down and enjoy making me.

Brooke Sykes (11)
Barlborough Hall School, Barlborough

A Recipe To Make Me

Ingredients:
8g history
1kg football
8g M&M's
2g animals
Splash of swimming
2kg chicken
2 eggs

Method:
1. Gather all the ingredients
2. First add a splash of swimming
3. Mix in 1kg of football
4. Crack the 2 eggs and stir
5. Whisk the 2g of animals, being careful not to get bitten
6. Sprinkle in the M&M's
7. Chop the chicken and add to the mixture
8. Finally, cook in the oven for 8 years and this is me.

Joseph Fuller (8)
Barlborough Hall School, Barlborough

All About Me

R   ight, I write with my right hand

I   love to eat chocolate chip cookies

Y   o-yos are my favourite toy

A   teddy was my birthday present once

N   o thief comes to my house

S   nakes are my favourite animals, too bad they are dangerous

H   i, my name is Riyanshi

I   have a brother called Divyansh.

Riyanshi Badhan (7)
Barlborough Hall School, Barlborough

How To Create Me

Get a scoop of helpfulness
Add a side of happiness
Pour in some sadness
Add a cup of sugar
Add a scoop of milk
Get 10 buckets of joy
Put a cup of funny in
Now stir 20 times
Bake it for two hours
Now stuff in chocolate
Then put in 12 candy canes
Next put cookie dough in
Then sprinkle with Roblox.

Zain Savage (8)
Barlborough Hall School, Barlborough

To Create Me You Will Need

One slice of humour
Three mixes of fun
A dash of serious
One pinch of interest
One pound of kindness
Measure a spoonful of loving
Next sprinkle being busy
Mix in some sport
Get a large bowl
Mix with three cups of fun
Place a pound of kindness in
Stir in the interest
Measure a spoonful of love.

Arjun Samra (8)
Barlborough Hall School, Barlborough

This Is Me

Add 10lb of football,
Mix in Bayern Munich,
Stir roughly while adding a slab of hot pepperoni
and jalapeno and cheese pizza,
Next, add a pinch of rugby,
Add a dash of games,
Spread the mix along the tray,
Cook until you see colours of blue and red,
Sprinkle on flags then leave to cool down,
This is me!

Leonardo Vögerl-Virgilio (10)
Barlborough Hall School, Barlborough

Amelia Ward

A melia Mae Ward.

M ental.

E nergetic.

L oving and kind.

I ntelligent and smart.

A ctive and fun.

W eird and crazy.

A good friend.

R espectful to others.

D etermined to reach my goals.

This is me, Amelia Mae Ward.

Amelia Ward (9)

Barlborough Hall School, Barlborough

All About Me, Tom

T otally good friend
O n the good chart
M uddy after football

W ant to always be a friend
E xcellent at naming animals
S uper at science
T errific at football
O rdinary chilled kid
N othing is bad about me

This is me.

Tom Weston (9)

Barlborough Hall School, Barlborough

This Is Me!

A large cosy bed, and I'll get out of your head.
I love the snow, I will run out and go.
I revolve around hecticness and happiness.
Give me popcorn in a cosy place
And you won't see me till the next day.
I am quick, I am fast
You might not see me sprint past.

This is me!

Leila Long (10)
Barlborough Hall School, Barlborough

Sport Is The Best!

Sport is my favourite thing to do,
Football, cricket and golf too!
Saving the goals on the field,
Maybe one day, we'll win a shield.
Bowling and batting, catching the ball,
Together we win, together we fall.
Hitting the golf ball off the tee,
Sport is my favourite and makes me happy!

Frank Jones (7)
Barlborough Hall School, Barlborough

This Is Me

F abulous at football.
O n my bed is comfy.
O bviously I am a pro footballer to be.
T otally good at napping.
B igger than a lion.
A fter a while, I get tired.
L ex is my name.
L ive life to the full.

This is me.

Lex Latham (9)
Barlborough Hall School, Barlborough

This Is Me

I adore ramen
I like light blue
I play the violin
I'm Chinese too!
Ducks are amazing
K-pop is too
My bias is Eun-Chae
She's Asian too!

I am like a cat
So now I am sat
Writing to you
So now hopefully
You know me too!

April Wang (10)
Barlborough Hall School, Barlborough

This Is Me!

T he best hockey player
H onest
I 'm as brave as a lion
S mart like a fox

I 'm a dancer
S o beautiful, like a butterfly

M e, I'm preppy
E ver so grateful... this is me!

Ava Bloomfield (10)
Barlborough Hall School, Barlborough

This Is Me

B rilliant at musical instruments
E ndlessly chatting
N oisy but in a good way
E nergetically funny
D oesn't like maths
I like Nirvana
C an sometimes be obsessed with screens
T alented.

Benedict Cross (9)

Barlborough Hall School, Barlborough

This Is Me!

M y favourite colour is blue
A pig is my favourite animal
T ea is amazing to drink
I like playing outside
L iving things are my best friends
D on't forget, I'm vegetarian
A nd what about you?

Matilda Farr (7)
Barlborough Hall School, Barlborough

William

W illiam is my name
I like to read at night
L ast month, I went to Dubai
L aptop is my best present
I love gummies and MrBeast chocolate
A hana is my mate
M y tooth fell out at school.

William Taylor (7)

Barlborough Hall School, Barlborough

All About Teddy

T iger is my favourite animal

E ating is my favourite thing to do!

"D ang it!" is my catchphrase

D odos were my favourite animal

Y o-yos are my favourite toy

W inning is my goal.

Teddy Wright (7)

Barlborough Hall School, Barlborough

This Is Me

I am kind
And have a good mind.
I am a football fan
And go to matches when I can.
I'm not tall
But I'm not small.
Everybody knows I love geography
I am world-wise and environmentally kind.
I am Thomas.

Thomas Waugh (9)
Barlborough Hall School, Barlborough

This Is Me

I am kind
I am fun
I am always on the run
I love pizzas
I love rabbits
And these things turn into habits
I am smart
I am small
And I know people can be tall
I love the way I am
And I'm a big fan
Because that's the way I am
This is me!

Eleanor Scholes (10)

Barlborough Hall School, Barlborough

This Is Me!

I'm as happy as a hyena
Kind as a kangaroo
Sometimes sad, like a baboon
Caring as a koala
Cautious like a cat
Generous like a dog
Quick like a cheetah
Mischievous like a monkey.
This is me!

Hugo Oliver (9)
Barlborough Hall School, Barlborough

All About Me

T ristan is my name
R ed is my favourite colour
I like football
S o what are you doing today?
T ristan is my name
A re you good today?
N ow, let's play football.

Tristan Carberry (7)
Barlborough Hall School, Barlborough

This Is Me!

I am kind
But my mind is small
Small for a boy with big dreams
I need to be small
To rule the supreme
Weird is my name
But football is my game
Cricket is not the same game
And will not be my claim to fame.

Jenson Wilson (9)
Barlborough Hall School, Barlborough

Who Am I?

Who is friendly but sometimes mad?
Who has two brothers?
Who likes video games?
Who is empathetic?
Who is happy and kind?
Who loves an adventure?
Who am I?
I'm Danny.

Danny Hollinshead (9)
Barlborough Hall School, Barlborough

All About Me

Q uinn is my name
U nique as a flame
I love pizza that is plain
N ever the same
N ever give up.

Quinn Ridgway-Coates (7)
Barlborough Hall School, Barlborough

The Elixir To Make Alice

Warning, this potion is only for the experienced and culinary magician; you have been warned...

You will need:
One teaspoon of honey,
A bit of money,
The fire of a dragon stuffed in a flagon,
A bowl of brown hair taken with care,
The bounce of a kangaroo with cartwheels for you,
Six diamond whiskers of kittens placed into mittens,
A splash of intelligent blue mixed with dew,
One cup of tricks followed by chicks,
One litre of maths,
Two handfuls of music,
The speed of a gazelle triggered by a bell.

Tools:
A teaspoon
A flagon
Bowl
Tweezers

Bucket
Jug
A new orange canoe
Piano and a guitar
Treble
Cauldron
Sieve
Spoon and a cup

Method:
1. Take the teaspoon of honey and let it slide gently into the cauldron (make sure not to leave the slightest bit on the spoon or Alice will be gone soon).
2. As a donation to this arduous potion add a bit of money (£5 would be good), place it carefully on the honey and stir till it turns to goo.
3. Use your bucket to splash the intelligent blue into the stew, but don't forget the dew.
4. Next, let the fire of a dragon burst out of the flagon. Like a firework let it spread out on all the sides of the bubbling, amber mixture.
5. Leave the clay to cool in a bowl for 10 minutes.
6. Add the whiskers of kittens in mittens and stir gently with a spoon until all that is left is 6 sapphire streaks.

7. For good luck (this potion can cause harm) release the multicoloured, exotic bounce of a kangaroo flowing with cartwheels for you.

8. At this stage, a small picture of Alice should appear in your blue liquid, if not, you have missed something out.

To perk up her looks, she will need a few crooks, So with tweezers, place her hair in a sieve with large holes. (Do take care with this delicate act or you will knot up the hair.) Shake the brown hair onto the head of the blue figure. With tweezers, adjust it into a slightly messy hairstyle.

9. Add one cup of the smartest tricks, don't forget the chicks.

10. From the jug, pour one litre of a mathematician, coming next, two handfuls of a grade one musician.

11. As fast as lightning, it can be frightening, set free the speed of a gazelle when you ring the bell.

12. Now Alice looks like Alice, but let's help her up a bit,

Jump into your orange canoe, make sure it's new, You're off to New York to catch a stork in the times of Guy Fawkes.

13. Finally, the piano and guitar, add the treble and you get a star!

This is me!

Alice Skinner (9)
Emmer Green Primary School, Reading

I Am Me

I am tired of being a pawn
In someone else's game
I am tired of being the one
Everyone seems to blame.

Yes I may be a little bad
But I am not going to change
You can say that I am weird
But what is so bad about being strange?

Yes everyone is different
But they can be who they want to be
Everyone has their ups and downs
And so do I, because I am me.

No one is perfectly perfect
No matter what you say
Even if you say I can't do it
I can, I can save the day

You can tell me I'm too weak
But I'm truly very strong

I am me and that's what matters
Not if I'm short or long

Yes everyone is different
But they can be who they want to be
Everyone has their ups and downs
And so do I, because I am me

Peer pressure and all that tricky stuff
Don't let it change who you are
You're you, they should accept that
You're one bright shining star

I am who I am
Even if they say I'm wrong
I can do this, I'll get through this
I know that I belong

Yes everyone is different
But they can be who they want to be
Everyone has their ups and downs
And so do I, because *I am me.*

Zoona Khizer (10)
Emmer Green Primary School, Reading

I Am Annabelle!

I am crazy creative in art and drama too!

A m I imaginative? Er, capital YES! Woohoo!

M usic is my thing because I love to dance and sing!

A mazing at badminton but sport's not my thing!

N ature is important so we need to play our part!

N ever give up hope and have a big big heart!

A nimals are cool but it's hard to choose just one!

B eginning friendships is my skill and making them last very long!

E nergetic, that is me bouncing around like a bunny!

L aughter is always near me, so I admit I'm really quite funny!

L ife at school is mostly a blast with a challenge here and there!

E veryone has a place in life on this great big planet we share!

Annabelle Taggart (9)

Emmer Green Primary School, Reading

My Pet

I see him every morning and he greets me with a
smile,
Then he tends to drift around, open-mouthed for a
while.

At breakfast he gulps his food, without a knife or
fork,
And when he finishes, he looks at me as if to say
please more.

He likes to gaze at everything and I wonder what
he thinks,
But when I ask him questions, he looks at me
without a blink.

He moves around so gracefully with no effort at
all,
I wish I could dance like that, but normally I fall.

When I play my violin, I ask him how it sounds
But he just stares back at me with an open mouth
as if to say "Wow"!

And when I say good night and go up to bed,
He knows there will be peace at last, as he smiles
and nods his head.

Sophia Smith (7)
Emmer Green Primary School, Reading

My Favourite Animals

I am fluffy,
I can make you smile,
Most people like me,
I am as lively as a chimpanzee,
I am not human nor monkey,
You can have me in your bed,
If you have no allergies,
I am slippery or scaly,
I am long,
And sometimes I have venom inside me,
Beware; I will not like you,
And try to bite you,
Do not go near long grass in Australia,
That is where I live,
I can grow up to seventy centimetres or seven metres,
There are 117 species of me in Oceania,
I can be a pet,
Or in the wild,
There are 345 types of me in the world,
I have a short, blunt beak,

I usually lay eggs,
I can live in trees or on the ground,
I have short legs with claws.

Theo Morgan (8)
Emmer Green Primary School, Reading

What Am I?

My hair is a pool of melted chocolate, trickling down my back with golden streaks of caramel.
My eyes are twin, raging, grey-blue oceans, each trapped in an orb.
My nails are swords, once were sharp now they are blunt, given away due to clashing teeth.
I'm like a jelly being poked, unable to keep still.
I'm a yelping dog, easy to disappoint but easy to cheer up.
My skin is a pale pink rose covered in snow.
My stomach is a huge tank, once you think you have filled me up, I find room for more.
Am I a chocolate fountain? Am I a sandy beach? Am I a small army?
Am I a quivering jelly? Am I a jumpy dog?
Am I a rose in a snowstorm? Am I an army's tank or maybe the world?
No! I am me.

Thea Hookham (8)

Emmer Green Primary School, Reading

Colours Surrounding The Town

Red is a title of anger,
The colour orange is vibrant and warm,
Yellow, as cheerful as the sun,
Yet jealous and silent,
Green fields, a whisper of resilience,
A silent sign,
Blue, a sign you are sad and left alone,
Purple, your own world inside you,
Violet promises in every dark cloud,
A silver line,
Indigo nights give a way to morning,
The rainbow is made out of weather,
Weather is winter,
A white blanket, soft and cold,
Spring, a palette awakens,
Summer follows with a bold fiery array,
Autumn whispers in shades of amber and red.

Meltem Bulut (7)
Emmer Green Primary School, Reading

Me

This is me,
And I am amazing,
And I fly, fly so very high!
This is me,
And I love the world,
The plants, the animals that buzz with life.
This is me,
And I love dogs,
Luna and Sunny are my favourites.
This is me,
And my friends are the best,
And we stick together forever.
This is me,
And I like cricket,
I'm good at batting, but not so good at bowling.
This is me,
And I rescue bugs,
And spiders and snails and slugs.
This is me,
And I am beautiful,
My eyes are bright and sparkling emeralds, my hair
is golden and glossy.

This is me,
And I love dragons,
They are majestic and awesome.

Lily Kilshaw (10)
Emmer Green Primary School, Reading

Moving Dreams!

In a world full of hope and endless skies,
Lived a little Isabelle with sparkly eyes.
She has not one, but two dreams so true,
She loves to dance and paint and that's what she will do.

From Monday to Friday, she'd spin and twirl,
Imagining cheers from every boy and girl.
But on weekends, something new would show,
With colours and brushes, she will glow.

Isabelle knows no limits, she would grow each day,
A dancer and an artist in her own special way.
So remember as you chase your dreams,
You can be more than one thing, or so it seems.

Isabelle Alvarez (7)
Emmer Green Primary School, Reading

A Recipe Of Me

You will need:
Two tablespoons of laughing and smiles
One dash of a little bookworm
Three tablespoons of beautiful
The tiniest bit of stubborn
A mixture of sweet and sour
One gallon of a beautiful voice
One dash of drama queen

First, get all your ingredients and pour them all
into a big bowl
(45cm tall)
Next, get some chocolate milk and pour it in
After that, mix well until you get a pink sparkly
batter with a little bit of teal
Then put it in the oven for two minutes
Finally, enjoy.

Naina Kalapala (8)
Emmer Green Primary School, Reading

Me!

A cting, dancing and singing are the best,

N o problems with friends because they're great.

N ice describes me and my school is nice too,

A mazing is a great quality, everything and everyone is amazing.

B eautiful nature means a beautiful world,

E ven though it's good to be safe you should still have adventures.

L ove, hope, joy and knowledge,

L ife, happiness, fun and caring.

E very day is worth it and you should celebrate yourself.

Annabelle Dunstan (9)

Emmer Green Primary School, Reading

A Recipe To Make Me!

A library full of reading,
A cupful of gymnastics,
A big bag of adventure,
A kilo of creativity,
A dusting of magic,
And a pinch of imagination,
Stir it all together...

Throw in a handful of happiness,
A million hugs,
A sprinkle of naughtiness,
A spoonful of smiles,
A drop of fun,
Finally, a splash of friendship,
Add your own touch,
Then whizz it all together!
You get me!
This is me!

Millie Rigler (7)
Emmer Green Primary School, Reading

What Makes Me Artistic?

A rt helps me create things that I and others can love and enjoy.

R unning keeps me fit and healthy.

T inkering things can make things more fun and better.

I nterior design helps me express my feelings.

S ewing makes me feel happy and free!

T alking helps me express my feelings and share my thoughts.

I deas are what power my creations!

C olouring helps me become mindful and calm.

Jasmine Lily Dixon (11)

Emmer Green Primary School, Reading

Creation Of Ingrid

If you are looking for a best friend, then make me!

You will need:
A sprinkle of naughtiness
1,000kg of kindness
100kg of helpfulness
100,000lb of adventurous potion

Steps:
1. First, add the sprinkle of naughtiness.
2. Then add the 1,000kg of kindness.
3. Mix, then add 100kg of helpfulness.
4. Finally, add 100,000lb of adventurous potion and mix until it becomes yellow.

This is me!

Ingrid Girjoaba (10)
Emmer Green Primary School, Reading

This Is Me!

Long brown glossy hair
With eyes like a rugby ball
Shy and quiet like a mouse
And neat fluffy eyebrows
This is me!

Painting is my favourite
Colours make me happy
PE isn't my favourite
Especially when it's chilly
This is me!

I like riding on my bike
And getting some fresh air
I love the fresh breeze
Running through my hair
This is me!

Zoya Ali (8)
Emmer Green Primary School, Reading

This Is Me

This is me,
I'm always happy as can be,
I like watching bees flying around the trees,
My favourite animal is a puppy,
My future dream is to have a boat and sail the sea.
When I climb my tree house and look at the sky, I
feel as free as a chimpanzee.
When I look out my little window and look at the
starry sky, I think of my good dreams and wonder
if astronauts are moonwalking there now.

Alec Morgan (7)
Emmer Green Primary School, Reading

This Is Me!

T he rushing of waves is what I like to hear,
H ugs, love and kindness help when I feel fear,
I n the mornings, people call me grumpy,
S ome days I feel jumpy!

I n my spare time I read,
S unshine is really what I need.

M aking memories with friends is fun,
E very time I do, I feel as bright as the sun!

Anna Bottoni (9)

Emmer Green Primary School, Reading

Hero

Once there was a girl who became a secret agent.
Aged 16, she travelled by herself to England from
Australia.
When the Second World War broke out, she joined
the French resistance in their fight against the
Nazis.
She was on top of the German's most wanted list.
The Germans nicknamed her the 'White Mouse'.
Who is she?

Answer: Nancy Wake.

Cerinda Sirichantaropass (11)
Emmer Green Primary School, Reading

Around Me

My name is Rahini,
I am very dreamy.
I dream about a star,
Because it is very far.
I like to eat noodles,
I also like poodles.
I like buns,
Because they are yum.
I have a friend called Dolly,
And she is very jolly.
I love to do gymnastic,
Because it is very fantastic.
I have a family of five,
And two of them know how to drive.

Rahini Didwania (7)
Emmer Green Primary School, Reading

This Is Me!

T ales and stories are my favourite
H ula-hooping is second best
I like dancing and also crafting
S inging is great and lovable too

I t is me who is a great friend
S ister who is always the best

M y lovely little bunnies jump around
E nergetic me kicking my football round and
round!

Sara Saoji (8)
Emmer Green Primary School, Reading

This Is Me

T o tell you what I like,

H ello, my name is Anna,

I love my family,

S o let me tell you some more.

I like sports like hockey and badminton,

S leep sometimes worries me as I have trouble getting to sleep.

M e, I really love writing poetry,

E lephant calves are very cute.

Anna Bhagalee (7)

Emmer Green Primary School, Reading

Me

C onstance is positive.

O thers aren't like me.

N ow I am seven!

S ome of my favourite colours are purple and pink.

T ea is my favourite drink.

A pples are one of my favourite fruit.

N ever call me Connie.

C onstance is kind.

E very picture I draw is special to me.

Constance Gillespie (7)

Emmer Green Primary School, Reading

How To Make Me

To make me you need:
Four bottles of happiness
Six spoonfuls of energy
Ten pinches of art and craft
A superb football player
One overflowing with ketchup hot dog
Two percent of being greedy
A bit of a healthy eater
One millimetre of sadness
And finally an excellent reader
This is me!

Leo Purnomo (8)
Emmer Green Primary School, Reading

This Is Me

I am a happy person, as kind as can be.
I like to play all day and night, I really am free.
I am a sporty person, I really, really am.
I hope you'd like to meet me as soon as you can.
I hope you are kind and nice and like to have fun.
You and me could play all day in the bright sun.

This is me!

Amy Grandison (7)
Emmer Green Primary School, Reading

My Opinion About Life

Life is hard, life is not fair,
There always will be a villain's lair,
Life is a torturing circle,
It is not always a chocolate truffle,
Life is a journey like a dart,
Going ahead and ahead everyone has a part,
You angle your dart to achieve your goals,
Winning or losing is not in your control.

Rudra Shembekar (9)
Emmer Green Primary School, Reading

This Is Me!

J e m'appelle Jessica.

E very day I do gymnastics.

S ometimes I do swimming.

S cience is one of my favourite subjects.

I have two siblings who are cheeky.

C amel stretches are hard, but I find them easy.

A pples are delicious.

This is me.

Jessica Swayze (7)

Emmer Green Primary School, Reading

Josie, Paddington Bear And Bruno All Stick Together

My name is Josie
I am nine years old
I have a Paddington Bear
Who comes with me everywhere
My favourite colour is pink
To make the boys wink!
I have a dog called Bruno
Who likes to play Uno
Josie, Paddington Bear and Bruno all stick together.

Josie Barnbrook (9)
Emmer Green Primary School, Reading

Flower Times

This is my poem called Flower Times
And I like dandelions
Like yellow lions
It will surely rhyme like every poem

Roses smell nice when you put them to your nose
Daisies are lovely when you are feeling lazy.

Isabel Sims (7)
Emmer Green Primary School, Reading

This Is Me

T he only thing I love is family.
H appy always.
I love Legoland.
S miley.

I love strawberries.
S omething to do.

M essy.
E xcited.

Amelia Singleton (9)
Emmer Green Primary School, Reading

My Life

R ania... This is my name, it's also my auntie's name. My dad named me after her.

A pple is my favourite fruit because it's red like blood.

N eon colours are my favourite colours because they are bright, that's why I like them.

I never give up in anything that's why I finished the PGL Adventure.

A dventure is the thing I like most. I did something called Survivor where we had to make houses out of wood.

S unshine is my favourite. I don't like rain, it makes you feel wet and I hate that.

L ong brown hair. I like my hair because it's so beautiful.

I ce cream in the summer.

F un day is Friday. I love Fridays so, so much!

E nd. This is the end of my poem. Did you like it?

Rania Abdelrahim (11)
Feversham Girls' Secondary Academy, Undercliffe

Daydream!

I crack my knuckles as I get out of bed,
Ready to start the day ahead.
Period one and two I feel weird,
Science is something I commonly feared.
Experiments about Bunsen burners,
Struggling to be one of Ms Miah's star learners.
Maths is a binary code of diagrams,
I don't know how to turn kilograms into grams!
Period three and four I hear at the back of my head
"Come on Arooj, two more hours and you're finished!"
That's what it said.
I daydream often about home and sleep,
But the journey to be a doctor is quite steep.
Heartbeats to injections are all that I like,
But sometimes it's a mixture of books and to write.
Poof, all that thought has taken me to the end of the day,
Now it's time to push the stress away!
Art is my home and life like biryani/rice.

Last bit of my day you should know,
My emotions can go above or below.
I want to be like her, the smartest person I know,
Who always answers a question,
And never gets a mark that is low.
My mum says, "It doesn't matter, you are you, she is she! Everyone is gifted in some way!"

So I try to be my best every day!
This is the end, I hope you had a lovely read-through.
One reminder is, people or a single person will still love you.

Arooj Iqbal (11)
Feversham Girls' Secondary Academy, Undercliffe

Breakfast

I wake up in the morning,
And head down to watch the telly.
But little do I notice,
The rumbling of my belly.
I stride to the kitchen,
For a morning meal.
Yet the only thing in the fridge,
Is a banana peel!
I sigh in disappointment,
And slump on the couch.
But I accidentally sat,
On my cat's tail.
Ouch!
It hisses with the same agony I feel,
Of not having my morning meal!
What is the time? 07:20?
I have lots of time until school,
Plenty!
Should I quickly pop to the shops?
Before all my remaining energy rots.
I have no adrenaline,

No mood, no feel.
Because I have not had,
My morning meal!
I trudge along an empty pavement,
Until I see something that strikes my amazement.
A corner shop,
Not too far from school.
Finally,
Something that will keep my cool!
I buy a bag of crisps,
Some juice and an oat bar.
Wait, let me check the time,
Whaa? It is 08:30!
They are going to give me,
A detention.
Unless...
I sneak in unmentioned.
No, that'll never work.
I give up,
I accept my defeat.
I drag myself home,
Fully beat.

I have bad luck,
My fate is sealed.
This is all because,
I have not had my *morning meal!*

Zaynah Hans (11)
Feversham Girls' Secondary Academy, Undercliffe

This Is Me

My name is Aliyah Mahmood,
My birthday is an amazing and fun day,
It is not like a normal day,
My family and friends come on my birthday,
My favourite colour is green and I think that is unique,
Green eye colour is quite rare, as most people don't have that eye colour,
My favourite day of the week is Saturday,
Because I don't have school or mosque,
I don't like Monday,
Because that is when school starts,
The food that I dislike is tomatoes because they taste weird and feel weird,
The food that I enjoy a lot is pizza,
Because it tastes nice and you can get different flavours,
My favourite animal is a dog,
Because dogs are cute,
I also like rats,
Eid makes me very happy because all my family gathers up.

Aliyah Mahmood (11)
Feversham Girls' Secondary Academy, Undercliffe

This Is Me!

A splash here, a splash there, see?
Gather the ingredients to make me!

First, add happiness, two pots full
Then add bossiness, two drops full...

Good vibes, let's go, woohoo!
And loving lots of that too!

A splash here, a splash there, see?
Gather the ingredients to make me!

A pen and paper defines my passion
A dictionary of words and a great sense of fashion!

Intelligence, ten drops in
Independence, pride, a dedication to win!

A splash here, a splash there, see?
Gather the ingredients to make me!

I like the rain, but not mud - ironic!
Cosy nights in are just the tonic!

A drop of mischief, a cup of love
I'm grateful for the blessings sent from above.

A splash here, a splash there, see?
You've found the ingredients, this is me!

Hawwa Ahsan (11)

Feversham Girls' Secondary Academy, Undercliffe

My Story Life

On 20th of June 2011,
A miracle happened,
A mother had given birth to her biggest dear,
A beautiful baby girl was born.

Later on in her life, she had many struggles,
But as time went along,
Through every hurdle,
Her parents, who are a wonderful couple, saw her through great struggles.

Two years have passed,
A wonderful blessing happened again,
Aisha was blessed with a baby sister,
Who was named after a famous date.

My life has become a lot more interesting,
And difficult, as I grow older,
Through the wonderful days, weeks, months, years,
But I am very grateful for every breath I take,
God has blessed me with a wonderful life and surroundings.

I am a strong, powerful, mighty loving girl,
But sometimes I wonder why I am here,
This is me!

Aisha Siddiqa (12)
Feversham Girls' Secondary Academy, Undercliffe

This Is Me!

Everyone is special in their own way,
Everyone, I don't need to explain, do I?
No two people are the same,
And never will be.
You and me are different,
But in a good way.
Have you ever seen two people who are the exact same?
I haven't.
This is me:
Me who is obsessed with reading and going for late night walks,
Me who tries to escape reality using music and likes drawing, writing and painting,
Me who is extremely claustrophobic and hates talking to people I don't know,
Me who prefers to stay quiet and hates being alone,
Me who is terribly afraid of the dark and really likes ferrets.
That was me,
And still is.

What are *your* likes and dislikes?
What about your hopes and dreams?

Arfa Tahir (11)
Feversham Girls' Secondary Academy, Undercliffe

The Horrid Homework

Oh no, we're locked at school,
With the teachers who think they are cool,
We're catching the bus that's always coming late,
We're rushing to class, I've sealed my fate,
I can't, I can't the teacher,
Wait... No! No! They're giving us homework, more and more.
I wish I could run through the door.
I don't want to do homework, I'm running away, but it's catching up.
Chasing after me like a vicious pup, phew!
Finally it's the end of the day,
The clouds are like me, grey.
I walk in and my mum says, "How was your school today?"
"You don't want to know," I said,
I wipe the sweat from my head, I sigh, "It's time for bed!"

Hawwa Nawaz (11)

Feversham Girls' Secondary Academy, Undercliffe

This Is Me, For You To See

This is me
I enjoy sports, which allows me to be free
Roaming full of freedom, just the thought fills me
with glee
If I give up, I feel as if I've committed a crime
In art, my biggest masterpiece makes me feel
sublime

This is me
Challenges always channel my inner resilience
Always showing my academic brilliance
I like having fun and I'm never austere
Sports can wear me out but sometimes I feel a
cheer

This is me
My imagination is colourful like the coral reef
Art can take time but when I finish there is no limit
to my gift
I don't care if I'm picked on or bullied
I feel like I'm sensitive and always get worried
This is me, for you to see.

Haniya Nazir (11)
Feversham Girls' Secondary Academy, Undercliffe

Behind The Mask

Another day,
Just the same,
This is what I always say.

I paint a smile
On my face,
Pretending that it's worth my while.

Keep up the act,
Happiness,
The only thing that I've always lacked.

Behind the mask,
"Are you okay?"
No one ever seemed to ask.

So many times,
I was left to rot,
Like a pair of rusty chimes.

I'm tired of pretending,
That my life isn't breaking apart,
Inside, I'm screaming.

Tears streaming down my face,
Just pull on the mask,
Don't leave a trace.

Boiling up like a flash,
Now I'm not alone,
Behind the mask...

Zakia Mohammed (11)
Feversham Girls' Secondary Academy, Undercliffe

Yes I'm Hifza

Yes, I'm Hifza,
Yup, that's me.
My name is Hifza Nadeem,
And I do like climbing or hanging on trees.
I live near a park,
I live near my friend,
We both like making up imaginative things on end.
We both like making books with each other, that is fun,
But now we're not close to each other,
Our sadness has won.
But I'm not alone, I still have more amazing people at my side,
Even though I still have contact with her,
So let me turn the tide,
Let me turn a chapter of my life
And let me write a new one.
I'll go far, trust me,
Just like the sun.

Now that this day is almost nigh,
My last and final word is
Bye!

Hifza Nadeem (11)

Feversham Girls' Secondary Academy, Undercliffe

This Is Me: How To Make Me

To make me, you will need to:

First add half a container of shyness powder (I'm very shy), two pinches of talking, a tonne of joy powder and stir well.

Next, you will need to find some tennis ball flour, and also a basketball.

Now for the sugary bit... you have to add some baking powder (it's a huge part of me).

Smaller than a teaspoon of unhappiness, because doesn't everyone cry?

For the final touch, you will need to separate the happiness eggs from the yolk and keep everything so neat.

It may become a Guinness World Record.

You have to add a diamond-like sparkle which can only be found in the forest of me.

There you have it, you have officially created me.

Amirah Hassan (11)

Feversham Girls' Secondary Academy, Undercliffe

How To Bake Me!

What you will need to create me:
200lbs of a fluffy white cat/kitten
A box of strawberries, just right and red (remember no seeds!)
A small chatterbox (aka *Me!*)
A hint of ire just for maths
A clay bead bracelet, just my colour
10lbs of fun and mischief

Now...
Get 200lbs of a fluffy white cat/kitten
A box of strawberries, just right and red
Mix roughly until it's as smooth as a table (remember no seeds!)
Measure it in a measuring tray
Sprinkle a clay bead bracelet, just my colour
Bake until soft and glazed
There just might be a few giddy bubbles
Just wait for it to cool down
There you have it...
A cake!

Leia Omer (11)
Feversham Girls' Secondary Academy, Undercliffe

How To Create Me!

To create me you will need:
A book-filled bedroom,
A handful of delicious, sweet cake,
15lb of joy and energy,
A pinch of mischief, with a dash of colourful
sprinkles,
A chunk of frosting.

Now you need to:
Add 15lb of joy and energy,
Mix in a book-filled bedroom,
Stir roughly, while adding a handful of delicious,
sweet cake,
Next, add a pinch of mischief, and a dash of
colourful sprinkles,
Spread the mixture neatly over a tray with baking
paper,
Cook until glazed and fun-filled bubbles can be
seen,
Add a chunk of frosting, and leave to cool down,
Now enjoy your scrumptious, tasty cake,
This is how to create *me!*

Ayesha Patel (11)
Feversham Girls' Secondary Academy, Undercliffe

All About Me!

This is a poem about me!
A little Muslim girl, starting secondary school
I felt like a suffocating fish in the air
As I was about to step in, I felt like my heart stopped
But after talking and talking, I made a lot of friends
My body felt at ease as the stress finally ceased.

The day finally ended and I felt splendid!
I went home to rest my aching bones
But I got up, as I remembered
I had to go to the mosque
I have never missed a day of mosque
As I knew I had to learn something
Two hours later, I came back
Smelling the fresh scent of chicken
I had my dinner and went to sleep
As I knew my journey had to repeat!

Hafsa Asif (11)
Feversham Girls' Secondary Academy, Undercliffe

All About Ayesha

A lways singing because of my bubbly personality.

Y ummy sweet tomatoes are my favourite food to eat.

E very time I'm sad my mum makes me feel happy.

S oft hands like a pillow and hair as black as night

H ugs are what I do best

A nd my dream is to be a masjid baji.

W inter is my favourite season because I don't have school.

A s I was walking one day suddenly five ducks crossed the road.

S unshine was bright like my ring.

E xcited in Feversham.

E vergy in the morning keeps me going through the day.

M y mum helps me with everything I struggle with.

Ayesha Waseem Attaria (11)

Feversham Girls' Secondary Academy, Undercliffe

Allah Is My Guide

Allah is my guide
He's always by my side
No matter the circumstances
No matter the hardships or challenges
I feel better when I think of him
Allah is my guide

I read dua and learn the Quran
And I fast during the month of Ramadan
My dream is that one day I will meet Allah
But I know that will only happen if I am good and
read my salah
Allah is my guide

He's with me when I'm happy
He's with me when I'm sad
He's with me even when I'm really, really bad
He cares for me with all his heart
He's cared for me from the start
Allah is my guide.

Anbar Saeed (11)

Feversham Girls' Secondary Academy, Undercliffe

We Are One

Roses are red, daisies are white.
I may not be perfect, but I am unique all right!
Believe it or not, I am confident and kind.
My plan is to help others, which takes a real mastermind.
The world may not be the place for me,
But I assure you that I will make it a place worthy.
My aim is to make a project 'we are one'
Do not judge me but many awards I have won
We are all brothers and sisters,
What matters most is how we treat others.
There is no black or white,
Skin colour means nothing, isn't that right?
My positive self and compassionate nature,
Will help me rise and build a future.

Zahra Ahmed (11)
Feversham Girls' Secondary Academy, Undercliffe

My Religion Islam

M y name is Mariam and my religion is Islam,

Y ou might think it is a waste of time, but let me explain.

R eligion to me is my identity, one of a kind,

E xploring and

L earning more about my religion,

I s what I do.

G ifted to wear a Hijab,

I s who I am.

O beying my God is what my religion shows,

N ot doing anything bad.

I slam is my religion, but also my pride,

S o this makes reading the Quran my guide.

L oyalty is key

A nd modesty too.

M uslims everywhere, one of them is me.

Mariam Khan (11)

Feversham Girls' Secondary Academy, Undercliffe

This Is Me!

To create me, you will need:
A bed full of cats
A pinch of fun and laughter
A dash of interesting books
A sprinkle of a divine dish
Five pounds of creativity
And a tiny bit of sweet and sour

Now you need to:
Add a mixture of cats
Drop in a bunch of interesting books
Stir until fluffy, like cats' fur
But not too rough
Spread evenly on the baking tray
Cook until glazing like caramel
Smell the breathtaking scent
Leave it to cool down
Can you smell the scent of fresh new books?
Feels nostalgic
This is me.

Inaaya Rizwan (12)
Feversham Girls' Secondary Academy, Undercliffe

This Is Me

T he happiest I can be right now

H appily playing and painting

I n this poem, the first two lines are clearly fake

S o fake, so obvious and such a lie, like how am I supposed to be painting right now?

I was kind of forced to write this poem

S lowly and trying not to get caught, I'm doodling a messy little drawing in my notebook.

M y stomach is aching for no reason

E , the letter E has to be at the end and I honestly don't know what to do with it. So just kind of deal with this line, I guess.

Huriyah Khan (11)

Feversham Girls' Secondary Academy, Undercliffe

This Is Me

A fearless knight
Wanting to fight
This is me
A subtle feather
Like glamorous heather
This is me
Serving others
To make them ecstatic
But failing
Like I'm pathetic
I aim to speak the truth
But my voice is cursed with lies
Inundated problems evolve around me
As if they're orbiting me
Hatred and love drown me to death
As if it's controlling me
Life is confusing
Like a rose which is blooming
This is me
A girl who fights for life

Like a tiger who roars
To fight for life.

Raihana Qudratullah

Feversham Girls' Secondary Academy, Undercliffe

This Is Me!

T rying new things
H aving fun
I nstant knowledge
S pecial person in my own way

I don't like bugs
S uper tired all the time

M ostly lazy like a sloth
E ducated

I like art
I like playing with slime
I like listening to music
I like drawing

This is me
What are you like?
What do you like?
What don't you like?
Remember, everyone is unique!
You don't need to change for anyone!
Don't forget!

Sofia Ali (12)
Feversham Girls' Secondary Academy, Undercliffe

This Is Me!

Kind-hearted and resilient
Awesome, super and brilliant
Loves science and geography
Not a fan of veg, especially broccoli
I love my faith, a guide to eternal peace
Love burgers and chocolate treats
My favourite thing is jewellery - bling, bling, bling
It makes me feel like a flower in the spring
I love my cat Kitty who is a ball of fluff and witty
I love my family and the bond we have is essential
I love me for me and that makes me special

That's me...!

Hibba Hussain (11)
Feversham Girls' Secondary Academy, Undercliffe

This Is Me!

I am one of a kind,
I am unique in everyone's eye,
I like communicating with God, loving my family
and adoring things that I love,
This is me being the one with extraordinary
feelings on the inside and the outside,
I am beautiful for who I am,
I would never change who I am,
I make people happy with my infinite feelings,
I always help others,
I always try, I keep marching,
I share my love and passion with my loved ones,
I am me and I would never change myself.

Areebah Ahmed (11)

Feversham Girls' Secondary Academy, Undercliffe

My Fluffy Adorable Cat

I am an 11-year-old girl
And I like playing with my cat.
I like cleaning and dancing.
My cat is ginger and he is very cute.
I feed my cat and I give him love.
He is so cute that I want to hug him like a teddy
bear.
He is fluffy and adorable.
My cat always makes me happy.
I love him and he loves me.
His eyes shine like a bright green torch.
When I stroke him his fur is as soft as a feather
and he starts purring
Which sounds like soothing vibrations.

Hawwa Ibrahim (11)
Feversham Girls' Secondary Academy, Undercliffe

This Is Me!

Unique inside,
My family is who I love,
My friends and I have a special bond,
Islam is my beautiful religion,
Kindness is who I am,
Happy outside and inside,
Allah is the creator of everything,
And I'm a British Muslim,
Reading is what I love,
Family is everything and Allah is who I pray to.
Allah made us,
Today is a good day.
I wear a Hijab, mosque is where I learn the Quran,
A cat and dog lover.
Hajj is where I want to go.

Umme-Khair Faatimah (11)

Feversham Girls' Secondary Academy, Undercliffe

This Is Me!

T his world is temporary, so I try and keep on my deen.

H ave many hobbies and goals to achieve.

I slam is the way of life, stick with it until the end.

S porty and smart, I try my best to hold a big heart.

I wish to be a doctor in my career.

S ometimes when life gets hard, I shed a tear.

M y family have been there to support me.

E ven if doors close, there's always a key.

This is me!

Sawda Zainab (12)
Feversham Girls' Secondary Academy, Undercliffe

Me

I am Halima Khan
And I originate from Pakistan
I always say salam
My true identity is Islam

I wear my hijab to cover up
Not only to pray but to hide my good looks
The Quran is my guide
And it's always by my side

I'm football crazy
That's why I'm not lazy
I love sports
It helps my thoughts
My favourite team is Liverpool
That's why I like football at this school
This is me and my identity!

Halima Khan (12)

Feversham Girls' Secondary Academy, Undercliffe

My Obsession: Cats!

Cats and kittens,
Some even the same size as my mittens,
So soft, furry and gentle,
My love for cats is very substantial,
Sometimes when I see a stray, I feel quite
overwhelmed,
All cats are very cute,
Some very shy and some even mute,
Cats make me happy whenever I am sad,
And cats cool me down whenever I am mad,
So there's no reason you shouldn't like those soft
little creatures,
Especially because of their tiny, adorable features!

Laiba Abas (11)

Feversham Girls' Secondary Academy, Undercliffe

How To Make Me!

Recipe:
A positive heart,
An enormous burger,
20lb of fun,
A pinch of kindness,
A sprinkle of beauty,
A fabulous family.

Now you need to:
Add 20lb of fun,
Stir slowly while adding an enormous burger,
Mix in a positive heart,
After, add a pinch of kindness and a fabulous family,
Then spread the mixture neatly over a baking tray,
Cook until crispy brown,
Finally, sprinkle a hint of beauty, and let it all cool down.

Hafsah Bismillah (11)

Feversham Girls' Secondary Academy, Undercliffe

All About Me!

This is me
I have hazel eyes and I love strawberry pies
I'm funny and kind, I hope you don't mind
My smile is as big as the river Nile
Islam is my religion, we read the Quran for our deen
Even though some of us would rather order from Shein
I'm half Bangladeshi and half British, that is my flag
Come with me to my home city with me and my fashionable bag

This is me
This is who I'll always be
I'm kind and caring, you'll see
My amazing personality.

Sajida Ali (11)

Feversham Girls' Secondary Academy, Undercliffe

All About Me

I know something special about me.
My favourite colour is green because I like
greenery such as the fresh air and the colourful
fruits in the trees.
My precious thing is my coffee.
When I drink coffee it relieves my stress.
In maths arithmetic is fun.
I want my life to be adventurous.
My favourite number is 2.
Facts about me...
I like to play football and cricket.
I am crazy and happy in my own life.

Aaidah Suhail (12)

Feversham Girls' Secondary Academy, Undercliffe

My Life

Hajira is my name and sleeping is my hobby
Even if I don't get any, I drag my body out of bed
Just to go to school and take a bunch of tests.
By the time I arrive home, I don't even have time to
say 'hello'
I eat and get ready and set off to mosque.
By the time I come home, it's eight.
I almost forgot, I have homework due tomorrow
Now that's another story for tomorrow.

Hajira Shehriyar (11)
Feversham Girls' Secondary Academy, Undercliffe

This Is Me

T his is what makes me
H ave many goals to achieve
I wish to succeed in my lifelong dreams
S imply because it's part of my deen

I slam is my way of life
S ometimes you have to thrive to survive

M y family and religion are keeping me up
E ven when times are tough, I never give up

This is me!

Aaila Zaman (11)
Feversham Girls' Secondary Academy, Undercliffe

All About Me!

My birthday, wow, what a brilliant thing,
Everyone likes it, especially me!
My favourite thing to do is ride my bike
It just makes me very happy.
Eid is the best,
Excited is the best feeling.
A roller coaster makes me very scared.
I dislike a lot of things such as tomatoes, chilli and
lots more.
Ice is cool on a hot day,
Sunny days are hot,
I like them.

Imaan Fatimah (11)
Feversham Girls' Secondary Academy, Undercliffe

Myself

My name is Aysha,
My hair is brown, big and wavy like a lion's mane.
My eyes are a portal, entering a distant world,
And I am as tall as a giraffe.

I am kind and sweet, like a little bird,
I have an amazing family,
They are the complete opposite of me.
Islam is our religion and my hijab is my protection.
This is me.
Aysha Memi.

Aysha Memi (11)
Feversham Girls' Secondary Academy, Undercliffe

This Is My Life

F avourite sport is football.

A lways wanting to play, hoping to be a footballer one day.

R esilient, never giving up, always trying.

E nergetic all day long.

E ntertaining is what I am.

H elping people all the time in return for an Aero.

A lways look up to my sister who is my role model.

Fareeha Ashraf (11)

Feversham Girls' Secondary Academy, Undercliffe

Football Star

F ootball on the pitch is my favourite game.
O utside playing feels the same.
O n the court I score.
T o be honest I want to win some more.
B allers try hard to shoot.
A mateurs try hard to float.
L and on their heads.
"L et me win!" he said.

Muniba Khan (11)

Feversham Girls' Secondary Academy, Undercliffe

What Makes Me Happy

K ittens and cats are my favourite animals.

H anging out with friends

A nnoying everyone is what people say about me.

D rawing is what I like to do.

I slam is my religion.

J umping on my trampoline makes me happy.

A nd lastly, I love to hear the sound of rain.

Khadija Javed (11)
Feversham Girls' Secondary Academy, Undercliffe

My Religion

My religion is Islam,
I follow the Imaan,
I pray on the masala,
My lord, who helped me, is Allah,
I pray to go to Jannah,
Smiling at people is sunnah,
I follow the five pillars,
Astaghfirullah to all of those killers,
To complete me, my religion takes a big part,
Which helps me to have a clean heart,

I love my religion!

Laiba Abas (11)
Feversham Girls' Secondary Academy, Undercliffe

A Recipe For Me

Joyful, caring, happiness and more is the recipe for
me
Throw in some fun, love and give it a stir
Mix in some caring chillies and turn the heat up
Add some cat-loving soup and let it soak
Sprinkle in some forgetful seasonings and give it a
last taste
Add the cracked eggs and mix it all together.

Ghaaziyah Rizwan (11)
Feversham Girls' Secondary Academy, Undercliffe

Me!

I like cats and love Boba,
I have one sibling and her name's Hania,
She's annoying and hates poems.
She always copies me and watches TV,
My mum's side lives in Pakistan and my dad's lives here.
My favourite colour is blue.
I like my friends and family too...

Zarrah Kabil (11)

Feversham Girls' Secondary Academy, Undercliffe

Recipe For Me

To create me you will need:
A pinch of dark humour,
A slab of kindness,
A dash of mischief,
A glob of chattiness,
A sprinkle of friendly name-calling,
15lb of fun,
Maybe 3lb more, just to be sure,
And finally a tech-filled bedroom,
With snacks just in case!

Youmna Hamed (11)
Feversham Girls' Secondary Academy, Undercliffe

I Am

I love to eat juicy chicken burgers.

N othing makes me more happy than my parents.

A bu gives lots of money on Eid.

Y ounger sibling always annoys me.

A ll day I bake cookies.

H arry Potter 'The Phoenix' is my favourite book.

Inayah Mahmood (12)

Feversham Girls' Secondary Academy, Undercliffe

Untitled

S ummer, my favourite season,

A nd this is my reason,

F riends all around me,

I am feeling free,

Y elling for ice cream,

A nd this is where I'm meant to be,

H i, I am Safiyah and this is me!

Safiyah Bint Ahmad (11)

Feversham Girls' Secondary Academy, Undercliffe

My Inspiration

My friends call me funny,
They always buy me lollies,
My favourite movie is Minions,
I can watch it all day and never complain,
I like juicy fruit with orange juice,
My favourite colour is pink,
When I see it I always blink.

Maryam Zeeshan (11)

Feversham Girls' Secondary Academy, Undercliffe

All About Me!

I love playing football,
It is my favourite thing to do,
I love to colour, as the world needs colour.
And I am very good at it,
My dream is to pass my GCSEs when I do them.

Marwa Nadeem (11)
Feversham Girls' Secondary Academy, Undercliffe

This Is Me!

F unny

A rt

T eaching

I ncredible

M arvellous

A rt.

Fatima Zahra (11)

Feversham Girls' Secondary Academy, Undercliffe

Whimsical Wonders

I ran, ran, ran - no thoughts in my head,
I saw his eyes and I saw red,
I saw the dark green leaves, I saw the beautiful
ridge lines in the bark,
Almost making shapes of wonders,
The trees I saw, that's what I was talking about,
They were like magic, it felt less tragic,
You might be thinking what was so magic, well it
was the branches,
They were leading me to him,
Through tears of desperation, I ran and ran,
Until I found the one, we bumped into each other,
We locked eyes for a second, a thousand daggers
raced through my heart,
Leaves fell beside us, shining in glee,
It was whimsical and wondrous, the seconds felt
like an eternity,
As I looked up...

Tiana Weston (10)
Ruskin Academy, Wellingborough

Spring

The sky is light blue,
The flowers are blooming,
The sun is shining.

Goodbye, winter,
Spring is in the air,
Flowers are in bloom,
You see colours everywhere.

The grass is green across the hill,
But yellow blooms the daffodil,
It's sunshine on a little stalk,
A friendly flower, I bet they talk.

Spring is here, spring is here,
Winter is gone and two flowers appear,
Three little robbins begin to sing,
Four bicycle bells begin to ring.

Spring is here,
And nature cheers,
As blossoms burst,
And shoots appear.

Twisha Patel
Ruskin Academy, Wellingborough

Harry Potter

There is a young boy named Harry Potter,
Who is not an otter,
He has seen a house elf named Dobby,
Dobby mostly has a strange hobby,
Harry has seen a boy named Draco,
He is sometimes mad like a volcano.

A wizard school called Hogwarts,
Has a House Cup award,
Everyone in this school is a wizard,
They can disappear like a lizard,
A girl wizard called Hermione Granger,
She is not a car, like a Range Rover,
Including one more boy, Ron,
He does not want to be a swan,
A wizard teacher, Professor Snape,
He is basically bigger than a grape.

Oliwia Dziecielska (10)
Ruskin Academy, Wellingborough

This Is Me

Today, tomorrow
And the next day after that
There will always be one me
And there is nothing truer than that.

But, what I love about myself
Is more than words can describe
But if I have to choose just one thing
As to what I love about myself
It'll have to be my caring heart
For those that I love the most.

C aring for others
A mazing at art
I ntelligent
R obust in learning
A ctive on the playground.

Caira-Jae Hill (10)
Ruskin Academy, Wellingborough

Family

Roses are red
Violets are blue
My family are awesome
Are yours too?
My mum's blonde
She has a magic wand
Does your mum?
Now, James Bond
My siblings are great
I don't have eight
My dad's name is Stu
He is cool when he goes out
He likes to play pool
My uncle is great and kind
He has a magic spine
He likes to rhyme
My nanny has a dog
And two birds
I love her more
Than two thirds.

Oceana Munton (10)
Ruskin Academy, Wellingborough

The Me Cake!

I'm baking a cake today,
In the month of May.
I will start with the bottom,
Because I've always forgotten.
Then we need the cream,
Before the bottom screams.
Then we add layers,
Just like football players.
But keep adding cream,
To make my smile gleam.
We put it on the top,
To clean it like a mop.
I will add the heart,
So it will not erupt.
The last thing that shall be,
Will be the word of me.

Patricia Zdrinca (10)
Ruskin Academy, Wellingborough

My Mum

My mum always helps me,
She is a great cook.
My mum is there when I am sad,
She always understands.

She is a great lunchtime lady,
She makes the line straight.
My mum always has a smile,
When my teacher tells her how good I am.

I feel safe when I'm around her,
She is one of my five to talk to.
When I am at home, she gives me a hug,
She likes the coastline.

James Coe-Welch (10)
Ruskin Academy, Wellingborough

Halloween

The night comes, Halloween begins
People are trying, kids are crying.
People are turning, people are hurrying
Love is then, love is nowhere.

Where clowns are coming, people are running
Halloween is a nightmare, asking people for candy
But it's not caring, people are there, people are
missing.
No one is listening, no one can escape from the
killer.
Ha, ha.

Martyna Grobelna (9)
Ruskin Academy, Wellingborough

Cats

Cats are cute and fluffy,
They can also be scruffy,
Cats are the best,
Though they can be a pest.

In all shapes and sizes, they come,
Cats think snuggles and kisses are fun,
Cats make really good pets,
And don't like to get wet.

They can be lions,
They play in dandelions,
They can also be tigers,
They are blocked by wires.

Maia Rickett-Browne (10)
Ruskin Academy, Wellingborough

Life In Summer As A Kid

Spring is new, summer is like a new white flower,
Autumn is spooky like a funny clown and winter is
old like an ice cube,
But summer is a dream, new school year.
The beach is warm for us to dive right in it, with a
big great smile.
It makes you happy, jumping on a trampoline, and
looking at the sun as it smiles to you.

Cleopatra Leon (9)
Ruskin Academy, Wellingborough

Autumn

Autumn is here and winter is near.
So let's put on our boots and go to the pumpkin
patch.
There are so many pumpkins!
There are big, small, orange, white and blue ones.
There are so many pumpkins!
I picked my pumpkin, so let's go home now and
carve my pumpkin.

Emri Johnson (8)
Ruskin Academy, Wellingborough

Ruskin

Ruskin's here! Ruskin's here!
We come in as people cheer.
People sing to us in sync.
As they do we blink! and *clink!*
Finally the gates open,
So we say goodbye to our friends
Whilst seeing a sports breakfast dodge in laughter!

Zyla Agyemang (8)
Ruskin Academy, Wellingborough

Cosy Cup

Leaves come,
Leaves go.
That's when you know autumn is here.

Sun goes down,
Gets really dark,
And all kids can't go to the park.

Cosy up and get your hot chocolate
As winter is on the way.

Lakiyra Morris
Ruskin Academy, Wellingborough

Autumn

Autumn is near
The leaves are changing colour
Now, it's getting cold
In autumn, you wear a fluffy onesie
The animals begin to sleep
You get to drink yummy hot chocolate.

Jessica-Rose Stiller (7)
Ruskin Academy, Wellingborough

Everyone Is Awesome

E ach day, I am positive

V ery thoughtful about others

E ven when the sky is grey

R emember to be kind

Y ou are fabulous

O nly good things happen to me

N ever doubt yourself

E specially when you're in PE

I love myself

S ometimes I can't believe my luck

A nd thank the universe for my blessings

W ith my family and

E very single friend

S ing happy songs

O r play football

M iracles come true

E nding my poem with a big thank you.

Leonardo Spurling (8)
Woodlands School, Great Warley

This Is Me, Demi B

D emi is a phrase that means king to me,
E verywhere I go, I move like a fast bee,
M aths is the best subject for me.
I love football and it will stick with me.

B asketball is not a good sport for me.
R est and health are important to me,
O rdinary is not me because I'm a king.
W inners are cool and just like me
"N ever give up!" is true to me!

Demi Brown (7)
Woodlands School, Great Warley

This Is Me, Fleur B

F lowers are my favourite thing,

L ovely, fluffy puppies are the things I like to see,

E xcitable is what my teachers call me,

U sually, you will find me playing with my Barbie

R emember that my family means a lot to me.

B eautifully me,

A mazing is what I try to be,

S uper-duper me,

I love school because it's fun for me!

Fleur Basi (7)

Woodlands School, Great Warley

This Is Me... Esmé

I love my family,
I love my cat,
I also love my cricket bat,
This is me... Esmé.

I am friendly,
I am ginger,
I run like a ninja,
This is me... Esmé.

I like to shop,
I like to draw,
I dislike it when my brother snores,
This is me... Esmé.

I love to love the world around me.

Esmé Burchell (8)
Woodlands School, Great Warley

This Is Me, Opalypopaly!

O utgoing, this is me!

P onies are my favourite, so is Timmy.

A nimals love me because I am cuddly as can be.

L eadership is my thing.

A ble is me,

D ogs are my favourite animal.

A pples are healthy for me.

M ummy means a lot to me.

S o I'm going to be me!

Opal Adams (7)

Woodlands School, Great Warley

This Is Me, Lucia E

L ovely flowers are my thing,

U sually out and about, can't you see

C old and chilly is not what I need, hot and sunny is where I prefer to be,

I like to be at my nanny's, feeling safe as can be,

A ll of my family is part of me.

E very day I'm myself, this is me!

Lucia Everson (7)
Woodlands School, Great Warley

This Is Me, Fantastic Chloe

C andy, I love, especially sour sweeties,
H appy is me, because I am always lovely,
L ovely as can be, with my family,
O h, how I love sports, especially running,
E xcited is how I try to be.

W henever I am sad, people make me happy.

Chloe Wedderburn (7)
Woodlands School, Great Warley

This Is Me, Izzy - Year 3

I am as lucky as can be,
Z ebras are the animal for me,
Z ante is the place to be for me,
"Y up, yup," my dog says to me and I say, "Oh
quiet down you silly bumblebee"

A lovely pupil I will be, because this is me!

Izzy Andrews (7)
Woodlands School, Great Warley

This Is Me, Adarsh V

A mazing is what I like to be.

D ogs are my favourite.

A nd I like hamsters.

R unning is fun to me.

S un is good for me.

H istory makes me happy.

V ery growth mindset is for me.

Adarsh Vemula (7)

Woodlands School, Great Warley

This Is Me, Timmy T

T idy as can be.

I enjoy hanging out with family.

M y family loves me.

M y mum and dad take care of me.

Y es, I love football because sports are good for me.

T eachers love me.

Timmy Tudor (7)

Woodlands School, Great Warley

Ranuka

R ed is my least favourite colour.

A wesome is what I am.

N ot being mean is what I like most.

U K is where I live.

K ind is how others describe me.

A mazing is what I want to be.

Ranuka Gunaratne (7)

Woodlands School, Great Warley

This Is Me, Kennedy

K ind is what I want to be.
E nergetic is how I seem to be.
N uggets are yummy to me.
N ever give up.
E lephants are cute.
D ogs are fun.
Y ou will love me!

Kennedy Cullen (7)
Woodlands School, Great Warley

This Is Me, Öykü

Ö ykü is so happy,
Y ear 3 is my favourite class,
K ind is what I try to be,
U nbelievable mermaids are my favourite thing to see.

Öykü Akcan (7)
Woodlands School, Great Warley

I Am A Snail

S low like a snail
N udged always
A ll I love to do is rest all day
I can be the best by me
L eave me alone, leave me.

Shreya Singh (8)
Woodlands School, Great Warley

This Is Me

I am me, a sucker for books,
Unique and quiet, you wouldn't be shook,
I don't follow, I'm no sheep,
I am crazy, although I love sleep.

I do things I like with happiness and pride,
In my heart, creativity resides,
I don't mind if I don't fit in,
I have six whole brothers who I would put in a bin.

I'm an Aries and I love the beach,
I'm super short so I can never reach,
I'm very odd and I like art,
My friends tell me I'm a little bit smart.

I'll be myself until the end,
Being me is my favourite trend,
With every step I'll leave my mark,
I am ten years old and I have a unique spark.

Abigail Thomas (10)
Ysgol Bryn Hedydd, Rhyl

How To Create Me!

You will need to create me:
Mixing bowls, one medium and one large
3 Welsh Dragon scales
A pinch of sweetness
A dash of cheekiness
500ml of dedication
Lots of hugs
5tsp of confidence
A sprinkle of happiness
A few grams of sadness
500g of kindness
750g of uniqueness
And a black belt attitude.

First, you will need to:
Add your Welsh Dragon scales to the 500g of kindness and your 750g of uniqueness into a large bowl and mix thoroughly.
Then add 500ml of dedication, a pinch of sweetness, a dash of cheekiness and a few grams of sadness to your bowl.
Mix and set aside your large bowl in the fridge, to cool for five minutes.

Add to your medium bowl, 5tsp of confidence, a sprinkle of happiness and lots of hugs, now mix gently for two minutes.
Next, take your large bowl out of the fridge, add your black belt attitude and mix for 30 seconds.
Finally put in the oven to bake for 45 mins. Take out when finished.
(Be careful! Remember to use oven gloves.)

Elin Mathews (10)

Ysgol Bryn Hedydd, Rhyl

Who I Am

I am me, not like the rest
Unique and special, I am blessed.
Creativity is the canvas for my creations
Art is the door to my imagination.

My eyes are diamonds, glinting with brilliance
I'm strong, with a bucketload of resilience.
My hair is the colour of autumn leaves
And in my heart, I always believe.

Memories, the story of my heart
Me and my family, couldn't permanently be pushed
apart.
Friendship, a universe beyond measure
But happiness is a treasure.

I'm helpful, I'm kind
I've got a super fast mind.
Maths and art is where I shine
But sport definitely isn't mine.

Determination is the fuel that keeps me going
But hope also keeps me flowing.

Anyway, this is me
I love being me with pride and glee.

Chloe Jones (10)
Ysgol Bryn Hedydd, Rhyl

This Is Me!

I'm me, odd, although quiet,
Shy and artsy, but I can cause a riot,
I am creative and I like to read,
In my own way, I plant my own seed.

I'm unique, and fairly smart,
I share my emotions through pieces of art,
I'm an actor and I'm a performer,
Being myself is always an order.

I'm an Aquarius and I love the beach,
I am super tall, nothing is out of my reach,
I adore colourful flowers,
Sitting amongst them for hours and hours.

I'm normally very energetic,
I'm me and I'm not apologetic,
With every step, I'll leave my mark,
I'm ten years old with a unique spark!

Sadie Schofield (10)
Ysgol Bryn Hedydd, Rhyl

This Is Me

I'm me, not like the rest,
Sporty and brave, I can be the best,
I don't cheat, I play by the rules,
In my own way, I don't suffer fools.

I wear my football kit with pride,
I'm a leader, I support and guide,
I don't fit in the mould, it's true,
Being happy is what I pursue.

I see the world in an action film,
I see the stars with a bright, brilliant shine,
I'm not a copy, I'm one of a kind,
In this world, I'm just a cool find.

I'm a tip-top performer,
I give off my best,
Being unique is my trend,
Zach is my name, a truly good friend!

Zachary MacClelland (10)
Ysgol Bryn Hedydd, Rhyl

All About Fabulous Freya

T winkling with mischief and glee,
H armony, the song of the natural world,
I dentity, a puzzle I piece together,
S elf-discovery, a winding path I explore,

I love nature and care for the Earth,
S cars, each one a mark of my resilience,

M y smile, a beacon of joy,
E mpathy, a border I cross to other hearts,

F riends, the stars in my night sky,
R espectable armour, I walk with pride,
E yes, like a dark grey,
Y outh, a treasure I shall hold forever,
A mbitions, the wind beneath my wings.

Freya Heeley (10)
Ysgol Bryn Hedydd, Rhyl

Whispers Of Wonder

Roses are red and violets are blue,
I'm as brave as a lion, it's true,
My luscious locks make me shine,
I'm as beautiful as a star in the night sky.

My eyes shine like the sun,
My teeth are as white as a star in the night sky,
A grin that can brighten any day.

A piece of my heart has been let into the world,
Friendship is a treasure beyond measure,
Memories stand in my heart,
Shine bright like the beautiful sea.

A ten-year-old girl walking across the clear sea,
A new identity found its path,
The sum of all that makes me, me.
This is me!

Lily Goddard (10)
Ysgol Bryn Hedydd, Rhyl

Finding Out My True Colours!

Friendship is something I'll keep forever,
Me and my friends are there for each other.
I love my family and my friends,
We will stick together until the end.
If you need me, just call my name
I will be there, even in the rain.

My eyes twinkle ever so bright,
They could guide me home any night!
My heart is a chest of happiness,
My eyes are my windows to my kindness.
Freckles full of courage and dimples full of
Secrets only I know.

A superstar striker,
And an amazing Ariel dancer

This is me, Lilly-May.

Lilly-May Bullingham (10)
Ysgol Bryn Hedydd, Rhyl

A Well Of Emotions

My eyes are the stars that guide me,
My smile is as bright as the sun,
My clothes are so colourful like a rainbow,
My hair is like a river
This is me!

The great leader I am, but oh so sweet,
Stars sparkle in my dreams at night,
You will never see me perfect because I am unique,
This is me!

When I open my eyes, I see a world so bright,
When I close my eyes, I see the moon so white,
I love my family to the moon and back,
My eyes are cobalt-blue waves, crashing against
the sand,
This is me!

Seren Jane Rastin (10)
Ysgol Bryn Hedydd, Rhyl

My Unique Me

T houghtful and fun
H appy and helpful
I 'm honest and kind and a
S uper good friend

I do love giraffes, as everyone knows
S ports too, keeps me on my toes

M y family and friends are special to me
E specially Hugo, who's as cute as can be

R ose is my name
O ne of my favourite colours is mustard yellow
S ummertime is my favourite time of the year
E yes like the shimmering sea.

This is me.

Rose Ashley (10)

Ysgol Bryn Hedydd, Rhyl

This Is Me!

I'm me, not always the best,
I try my hardest to keep up with the rest,
Caring for others, I like to please,
In my own way, that's how I lead.

I look forward to the future,
Let's see where we'll go,
An artist is what I would love to be,
Fingers crossed, let's wait and see.

I see the world, happy and free,
Stars sparkle in the night sky,
I'm not a clone, I'm very kind,
In this huge world, I'm here to shine!

Erin Smith (10)
Ysgol Bryn Hedydd, Rhyl

This Is Me!

Happy, blessed,
Always trying harder than the rest,
Geography is my brain diet,
Whilst art is a complete riot!

I bike, I ride,
I swim over the treacherous tide,
A laser cutter lover, a chocolate chomper,
Being a head boy, I'm a bully stomper.

I'm always Dylan, Dylan Bailey,
Someone is always ready to save me,
Happy, sad, whatever I feel,
I'm always proud, I'm the next big deal!

Dylan Bailey (10)
Ysgol Bryn Hedydd, Rhyl

This Is Me

I am me and no one else,
I love playing football and going out,
I am a loving, caring and supportive friend,
I love playing football to the end,
I play for NFA like anyone else,
I am lightning in my tennis shoes,
I am as funny as a hyena,
I am a good footballer with a powerful shot,
I am always making my friends laugh,
I am a super tennis player on the court,
This is me.

Jacob Bellis (11)
Ysgol Bryn Hedydd, Rhyl

 YoungWriters® — Est. 1991 —

YOUNG WRITERS INFORMATION

We hope you have enjoyed reading this book – and that you will continue to in the coming years.

If you're the parent or family member of an enthusiastic poet or story writer, do visit our website www.youngwriters.co.uk/subscribe and sign up to receive news, competitions, writing challenges and tips, activities and much, much more! There's lots to keep budding writers motivated!

If you would like to order further copies of this book, or any of our other titles, then please give us a call or order via your online account.

Young Writers
Remus House
Coltsfoot Drive
Peterborough
PE2 9BF
(01733) 890066
info@youngwriters.co.uk

Join in the conversation!
Tips, news, giveaways and much more!

 YoungWritersUK YoungWritersCW youngwriterscw

 Scan me to watch the This Is Me video!